# Ace Your Job Hunt In Japan:
# Tips From A Recruiter

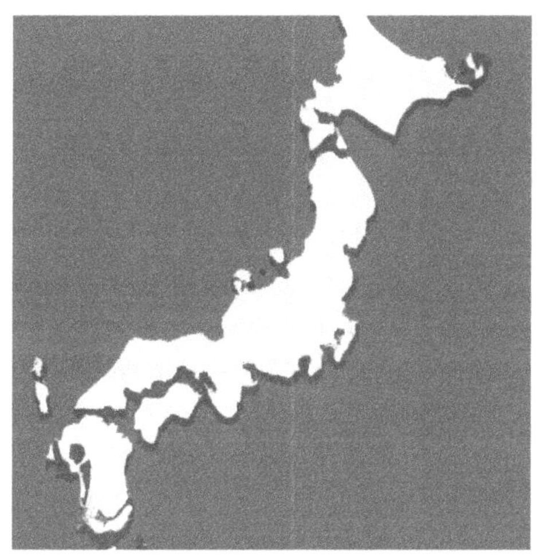

Written by Tokyo Paul

**Social Media Sites (SNS)**

YouTube: https://www.youtube.com/@TokyoPaul

Instagram: https://www.instagram.com/tokyopaullive

Twitter: https://twitter.com/tokyopaullive

Facebook:

https://www.facebook.com/groups/tokyopaul (groups)

https://www.facebook.com/TheTokyoPaul (page)

Website: https://TokyoPaul.com

## Acknowledgements

I want to convey my sincere appreciation to the viewers of my YouTube channel Tokyo Paul, who gave me support and motivation when I was working on this project. This book would not have been possible without their support.

I also like to express my gratitude to my wife for her help. Her invaluable feedback and support were essential in making this idea a success.

I want to thank my family, friends, and readers one more time for their kindness and support. Thank you to everyone from the bottom of my heart!

## Chapter One

## An Introduction to Job Hunting in Japan and the purpose of this book

Job seeking in Japan is a complicated process that involves much planning and study. If you intend to seek for work in Japan, it is critical that you grasp the country's job-hunting culture and conventions. This book will provide you a complete insight of the job search process in Japan.

Another important aspect of job hunting in Japan is the emphasis on group interviews and assessments. Companies often invite multiple candidates to attend interviews and assessments together. This approach allows companies to evaluate not only individual skills but also teamwork and communication abilities.

The purpose of this book is to provide job seekers with valuable insights and tips for navigating the job market in Japan. I have witnessed firsthand how challenging it can be for foreign job seekers to find employment in the country. Therefore, this section aims to equip readers with the necessary knowledge and strategies to increase their chances of success in their job search.

In this book, readers will find a complete guide to job hunting in Japan, which includes information on the Japanese job market, cultural norms and expectations in the hiring process, and common challenges faced by foreign job seekers. Additionally, readers will learn about effective job search strategies, such as networking, utilizing job sites, and making a strong impression during the interview process.

The tips provided are based on my personal experience as a recruiter, as well as insights from other industry professionals. By following the advice outlined, readers will be better prepared to navigate the job market in Japan and increase their chances of finding fulfilling employment.

**Who is This Book For**

Job seeking in Japan may be difficult, especially if you are new to the country or are inexperienced with the Japanese labor market. This book aims to provide you with a comprehensive guide on how to navigate the job search process in Japan, from creating a winning resume to acing the interview and landing your dream job.

The book covers a range of topics that are essential to any job seeker in Japan. It starts by introducing you to the Japanese job market, providing insights into the industries, and types of companies that hire in Japan. You will learn about the importance of networking and building connections in Japan, as well as the cultural differences that may come up during the job search process.

The book will next walk you through the resume writing process. You will learn how to write a Japanese-style resume that displays your talents and experiences in a way that Japanese companies would like. The book will guide you on how to write a great resume and cover letter, as well as how to adjust your application materials to specific job listings.

Once you have your application materials ready, the book will show you how to search for job openings in Japan and apply for them. You will learn about the different job search platforms that are popular in Japan, as well as the best ways to follow up with potential employers.

The book will also provide detailed instructions on how to prepare for job interviews in Japan, such as what to wear, what to bring, and how to answer typical interview questions. You will learn about the cultural nuances of interviewing in Japan and how to make a positive impression on your potential employer.

In addition to job search strategies, the book will provide you with insights on how to handle common challenges that job seekers face in Japan, such as language barriers and cultural differences. You will learn how to overcome these challenges and position yourself as a strong candidate for your desired job.

Finally, the book will provide you with tips on how to succeed in your job once you have landed it. You will learn about Japanese work culture and how to adapt to it, as well as strategies for building relationships with your colleagues and advancing your career in Japan.

The book also covers topics such as work-life balance and job security, which are important considerations for anyone working in Japan.

Overall, this book is a comprehensive guide to job hunting in Japan. It provides practical advice and insights on every aspect of the job search process, from resume creation to interview preparation to career advancement. Whether you are a foreigner or a Japanese national, this book will equip you with the tools you need to succeed in your job search and thrive in your career in Japan.

**Benefits of Working in Japan**

Japan provides a unique and rewarding experience for those who choose to work there. These are a few advantages of working in Japan:

**Job Security**

Japanese companies are known for their strong commitment to job security. Once an employee is hired, they can expect to enjoy long-term employment and the benefits that come with it, such as healthcare, retirement plans, and paid vacation time. This strong commitment to job security is one of the reasons why many people choose to work in Japan. It provides a sense of stability and security that is hard to find in other countries.

**Cultural Experience**

Working in Japan offers the opportunity to experience a unique and fascinating culture. From the food and fashion to the art and architecture, Japan has a rich and diverse cultural heritage that is sure to captivate and inspire. The Japanese people are known for their hospitality and welcoming nature, and this is reflected in the workplace. Many companies offer cultural exchange programs and language classes to help employees learn more about the culture and language.

**Language Skills**

Working in Japan is an excellent method to acquire and enhance your Japanese language abilities. The Japanese language is among the most difficult to learn, but it is also among the most rewarding. Learning able to speak and comprehend Japanese can open doors to new opportunities and help you interact with colleagues and clients. Several workplaces

provide language programs to help employees improve their language

skills, and there are numerous private language schools available for

those who want to take their language studies to the next level.

# Chapter Two

# Understanding the Job Market & Work Culture in Japan

## Japan's Labor Market Situation

Japan is one of the world's largest and most sophisticated economies, noted for its technological advances. The country boasts a highly trained labor force in a variety of industries. The Japanese labor market has been reasonably steady in recent years, with unemployment rates averaging around 2.5%.

## Industries That Are Expanding

Several industries in Japan are experiencing significant growth, presenting numerous job opportunities for skilled workers. The following are some of the sectors that are expanding in Japan:

**Information Technology**

Japan has to some of the world's most imaginative and successful technical enterprises. The country's robust IT sector is quickly increasing, fueled by the expansion of the digital economy. With rising demand for technology-related services, Japan is in desperate need of experienced IT experts. Since technology connects the world, Japan has been fast to embrace digital innovation, and the IT industry is likely to develop in the future years.

**Healthcare**

Japan's aging population has resulted in a huge increase in demand for healthcare services. As a result, Japan's healthcare business is quickly developing. The country need medical personnel such as physicians, nurses, and carers. Furthermore, Japan is investing in innovative technology and therapies to enhance the health of its inhabitants. This involves the creation of new pharmaceuticals, medical equipment, and other forms of healthcare technology. As a result, demand for healthcare professionals is likely to increase in the future years.

**Renewable Energy**

Japan is striving hard to transition away from nonrenewable energy sources and toward more sustainable alternatives. The government is investing extensively in renewable energy, which has resulted in industrial growth. Engineers and technicians are especially in great demand in this area. Japan has set a target of producing 22-24% of its energy from renewable sources by the year of 2030, and the government has enacted legislation to support the growth of the renewable energy industry. As a result, the need for professionals in this industry is expected to grow further in the coming years.

**Tourism**

The tourism industry in Japan is also on the rise. Japan has become a popular travel destination for people all around the world. The country's unique culture, delicious food, and beautiful scenery have attracted many tourists. As a result, the tourism industry in Japan is expanding, providing numerous job opportunities for those with language and hospitality skills.

## Robotics

For many years, Japan has been at the forefront of robotics technology. The government is substantially investing in the development of robots technology, which has resulted in the industry's growth. Professionals in this field, particularly engineers and technicians, are in great demand. The robotics business is predicted to increase in the next years due to the rising need for automation in numerous industries.

## Types of Jobs

The job sites mentioned above offer various types of jobs, including teaching, IT, engineering, finance, marketing, and hospitality. There are also opportunities for mid to senior-level positions in various industries. Whether you are a recent college graduate looking for an entry-level position or an experienced professional looking for a mid to senior-level position, there are job opportunities available for you in Japan.

**IT Jobs vs. English Teaching Jobs in Japan**

Japan has become a popular destination for foreigners seeking job opportunities, especially for English teachers and IT professionals. With its unique and rich culture, top-notch technology and advancements in different fields, Japan offers a wide range of job opportunities for people from all over the world.

Job hunting in Japan can be difficult for people who are new to the country, particularly if they do not understand Japanese. This section will explain the distinctions between looking for IT employment and English teaching positions in Japan, as well as the web tools and companies that may assist you with your job search.

**IT Jobs**

Japan is known for its advanced technology, making it a hub for IT jobs. The IT industry in Japan is always in need of skilled professionals, specifically in the areas of software development, web design, and system engineering. However, finding an IT job in Japan may be challenging, especially for those who do not speak Japanese.

**English Teaching Jobs**

There are several chances for anyone interested in teaching English in Japan. English teaching jobs in Japan range from instructing youngsters at private language schools to instructing adults in corporate English. The job search procedure, however, may differ from that of IT positions.

## Skills That Are in Demand

The job market in Japan is highly competitive, and job seekers need to possess in-demand skills to secure employment. The following are some of the skills that are currently in demand in Japan:

## Language Abilities

Language skills, particularly English competence, are highly valued in Japan. English proficiency is highly valued in a number of fields, including finance, information technology, and tourism. Additionally, as Japan's global connectedness expands, so does the demand for personnel fluent in other languages such as Chinese and Korean.

## Technological Knowledge

As Japan's IT and robotics industries expand, there is a great need for technological personnel. This covers programming, web development, and data analysis skills. Furthermore, as Japan invests in emerging technologies like as artificial intelligence and the Internet of Things, the demand for people who can create and execute these technologies is increasing.

**Healthcare Skills**

As previously mentioned, Japan's healthcare industry is expanding, and there is a growing demand for healthcare professionals. This includes skills such as medical knowledge, caregiving, and nursing. In addition, as Japan invests in new healthcare technologies, there is a growing need for professionals who can develop and implement these technologies.

**Hospitality Skills**

With the rise of tourism in Japan, there is a growing demand for professionals with hospitality skills. This includes skills such as customer service, communication, and cultural awareness. In addition, as the tourism industry becomes more competitive, there is a growing need for professionals who can offer unique experiences to visitors.

## Salaries in Japan

When it comes to job hunting in Japan, one of the most critical factors is salary. The country has a reputation for offering high-paying positions, but the reality is more complex. In this book, we'll explore salaries in Japan from a recruitment perspective, including some actual salaries in yen and US dollar equivalents.

## Average Salaries

According to data from the Ministry of Health, Labour and Welfare, the average annual salary in Japan is around 4.14 million yen. This equates to roughly $38,000 in US dollars. However, this figure varies significantly depending on the industry, company size, and location.

The average salary in Japan is higher than in many other countries, but it is important to note that the cost of living in Japan is also higher, particularly in major cities. Therefore, it's crucial to consider the cost of living when evaluating job offers in Japan.

**Salaries by Industry**

Some industries in Japan offer higher salaries than others. For example, the IT sector is known for providing competitive pay to attract top talent. In contrast, the hospitality industry may offer lower salaries due to the nature of the work.

Below are some average salaries by industry for mid-career professionals (with 5-10 years of experience):

- IT: 7-10 million yen ($65,000-$93,000)

- Finance: 6-9 million yen ($56,000-$84,000)

- Consulting: 7-10 million yen ($65,000-$93,000)

- Manufacturing: 5-8 million yen ($47,000-$75,000)

- Education: 4-6 million yen ($37,000-$56,000)

It's important to keep in mind that these are general averages, and salaries can vary widely depending on the specific position, company, and region. For example, a software engineer at a large technology company in Tokyo may earn significantly more than an IT professional in a smaller city.

**Salaries by Company Size**

The size of a company can also impact salaries in Japan. Larger companies with more resources may offer higher salaries to attract top talent. However, smaller companies may offer other benefits, such as a more flexible work schedule or a greater opportunity for professional development.

Below are some average salaries by company size:

Large corporations: 6-10 million yen ($56,000-$93,000)

Medium-sized companies: 5-8 million yen ($47,000-$75,000)

Small businesses: 3-5 million yen ($28,000-$47,000)

Again, it's important to note that these are general averages, and salaries can vary widely depending on the specific company and industry.

**Salaries by Location**

Location also plays a significant role in salaries in Japan. Major cities like Tokyo and Osaka tend to offer higher salaries due to the higher cost of living. However, some rural areas may offer lower salaries due to the lower cost of living.

**Below are some average salaries by location:**

- Tokyo: 6-10 million yen ($56,000-$93,000)

- Osaka: 5-8 million yen ($47,000-$75,000)

- Rural areas: 3-5 million yen ($28,000-$47,000)

It's important to consider the cost of living when evaluating job offers in different locations in Japan. While salaries may be higher in major cities, the cost of living may also be significantly higher, meaning that the overall financial benefit may not be as significant.

**Challenges Faced By Job Seekers in Japan**

Japan's unique culture and language can make it difficult for foreigners to find work in the country. Here are some of the challenges foreigners face when job hunting in Japan.

Japanese is a complex language, and while many Japanese companies require fluency in Japanese, many foreigners struggle to achieve this level of proficiency. This can make it challenging to communicate with potential employers or understand job requirements.

Japanese culture is vastly different from that of many Western countries, and foreigners may struggle to navigate cultural nuances during job interviews or in the workplace. For example, Japanese companies place a strong emphasis on teamwork and group harmony, which can be difficult for foreigners who are used to more individualistic work environments.

Foreigners who wish to work in Japan must obtain a work visa, which can be a lengthy and complicated process. Additionally, the Japanese government places strict requirements on residency, which can make it challenging for foreigners to find affordable housing near their workplace.

Despite these challenges, many foreigners still find success in Japan's job market. With determination, language skills, and a willingness to adapt to cultural differences, job seekers can overcome these obstacles and find fulfilling careers in Japan.

**Japanese Work Culture and Etiquette**

Japan has a unique work culture and etiquette that is deeply rooted in their history and culture. It is important to understand and respect these customs when working or doing business in Japan.

**Work Culture**

In Japan, work is highly valued and employees are expected to be dedicated and hardworking. Punctuality is also a key aspect of Japanese work culture, so it is important to arrive on time for meetings and appointments. Being late to a meeting or appointment is considered a sign of disrespect in Japan, and it can negatively affect your reputation.

Another important aspect of Japanese work culture is the emphasis on teamwork and harmony. Employees are expected to work together towards a common goal and to prioritize the needs of the group over individual needs. This means that decision-making is often done through consensus-building rather than individual initiative. It is also common for colleagues to socialize outside of work hours to build stronger relationships and foster a sense of camaraderie.

In addition, the concept of "lifetime employment" is still prevalent in Japan. Many Japanese companies offer job security and opportunities for career advancement to their employees as long as they remain loyal and dedicated to the company.

**Business Etiquette**

While conducting business in Japan, it is critical to understand correct manners. These are some crucial items to remember:

**Business Cards**

Business cards are a big deal in Japan. Always bring plenty of business cards and be sure to present them with both hands. When receiving a business card, take a moment to read it carefully and show respect to the person who gave it to you. It is also common to bow slightly when exchanging business cards.

**The Role of Universities**

In Japan, universities play a significant role in the job-hunting process. Many companies target specific universities, and students are expected to start their job search early in their final year. This means that job fairs and company presentations are common on campus, and students are expected to submit their resumes and attend interviews well before graduation.

The early start is because of the structured job-hunting process known as "Shushoku Katsudo." This process involves students undertaking job hunting activities in their final year of university, which is highly structured, including researching companies, attending job fairs and company presentations, submitting resumes, and attending interviews. The process can be pretty competitive, and many students spend a considerable amount of time and effort preparing for it.

# Chapter Three

# Japanese Language Skills are Important for Japan

Learning Japanese can be a valuable skill that can benefit you in many ways. The following are some reasons why Japanese language skills are important.

If you work in a global company or want to do business with Japanese companies, having Japanese language skills can give you a competitive edge. Japan is a world leader in technology, business, and innovation. Many global companies have branches or partnerships in Japan, and knowing the language can give you an advantage in communication and building relationships.

Japan is a popular tourist destination with a rich culture and history. Knowing Japanese can make your travels much easier and more enjoyable. You'll be able to navigate the country with ease, interact with locals, and fully immerse yourself in Japanese culture.

Learning Japanese can help you understand and appreciate Japanese culture, from traditional customs to modern pop culture. You'll be able to read Japanese literature, watch Japanese movies and TV shows without subtitles, and understand the nuances of Japanese humor and social customs.

Improving your Japanese language skills can be challenging, but it doesn't have to be. The following are some tips that may be helpful to you. Consistent practice is key to improving your language skills. Set aside time every day to study and practice Japanese. This can be as simple as reviewing vocabulary, listening to Japanese music, or watching a Japanese TV show.

**Tips for Improving Your Language Skills**

Surround yourself with Japanese language and culture as much as possible. Watch Japanese movies and TV shows, listen to Japanese music, and read Japanese books and articles. You can also join Japanese language groups on social media to connect with other learners and native speakers.

Find someone who speaks Japanese and is learning your native language. You can practice speaking with each other and help each other improve. This is a great way to get feedback on your pronunciation and grammar, as well as learn more about Japanese culture from a native speaker.

There are many language learning apps that can help you improve your Japanese skills. Some popular ones include Duolingo, Rosetta Stone, and Memrise. These apps are designed to make language learning fun and accessible, with features like gamification, speech recognition, and interactive exercises.

**Resources for Learning Japanese**

There are many resources available for learning Japanese, both online and offline. Here are some of the most popular resources for you.

Language schools offer in-person and online classes for learners of all levels. These schools employ experienced teachers who can provide personalized instruction and feedback. One school I have used in the past is Coto Japanese Academy - Japanese Language School located in Tokyo, https://cotoacademy.com/.

In addition to language learning apps, there are also apps specifically designed for learning Japanese, such as Kanji Study and Human Japanese. I have used the app Flashcards, which does cost a small fee, to help me memorize Japanese words. These apps offer features like flashcards, quizzes, and reading practice to help you improve your Japanese skills.

# Chapter Four

# Preparing Your Resume and Cover Letter

If you're planning to apply for a job in Japan, it's essential to understand the differences between the two main types of resumes used in the country - Rirekisho and Shokumukeirekisho. Each type of resume has its own format, purpose, and level of detail, and choosing the right one can make a significant impact on your job application success.

**The Rirekisho**

The Rirekisho is a basic type of Japanese resume that's commonly used by applicants for part-time jobs or entry-level positions. It's a one-page document that contains personal information, educational background, work experience, and skills. This type of resume is usually handwritten in black ink and can be bought from convenience stores or printed from the internet.

**How to Write a Rirekisho Japanese Resume**

A resume is known as a Rirekisho in Japan. It is a necessary document for the job application procedure. The following are the stages to writing a Rirekisho.

**Step 1: Choose the Right Format**

There are two types of Rirekisho formats: the Shokumukeirekisho and the Rirekisho. The Shokumukeirekisho is the most commonly used. It is a basic resume that includes your personal information, educational background, work experience, and skills. The Rirekisho is a more detailed version of the Shokumukeirekisho.

## Step 2: Personal Information

The first portion of your Rirekisho should include your personal information, namely your name, address, phone number, and email address. It is vital to provide accurate information.

## Step 3: Educational Background

In this section, you should list your educational background starting with the most recent. Include the name of the school, the degree obtained, and the date of graduation.

## Step 4: Work Experience

List your work experience starting with the most recent. Include the name of the company, your job title, the dates of employment, and your job duties. Be sure to highlight your achievements and accomplishments.

**Step 5: Skills**

List your skills that are relevant to the job you are applying for. Include computer skills, language skills, and any other skills that may be relevant.

**Step 6: References**

Include at least two references. Provide their names, job titles, and contact information.

**Step 7: Review and Edit**

Review your Rirekisho to ensure that it is error-free. Edit it for clarity and consistency.

Resume #1 – Rirekisho（履歴書）– Japanese Version

# 履 歴 書

2023 年1 月1 日現在

| ふりがな | やまだたろう |
|---|---|
| 氏 名 Name | 山田 太郎 |

| 国籍 Natinoality | 日本 | 生年月日（年齢）Birth | 1980年 月 1日1生（満 43 歳） | 性別 Sex | 男 ・ 女 |

| ふりがな | とうきょうとしぶやくじんぐうまえ1-1-1 |
|---|---|
| 現住所 Address | 〒<br>東京都渋谷区神宮前1-1-1 |
| ふりがな | |
| 連絡先 | 〒 |

電話 Phone
090-1234-5678
メールアドレス Email
taroyamada@example.com
電話
メールアドレス

| 年 Year | 月 Month | 学 歴 ・ 職 歴 （各別にまとめて書く）Education and Work History |
|---|---|---|
| | | 学 歴 Education |
| 2000 | 4 | 大学：東京大学工学部電気工学科 - 学位：学士（工学）入学 |
| 2004 | 3 | 大学：東京大学工学部電気工学科 - 学位：学士（工学）卒業 |
| | | |
| | | 職 歴 Work History |
| 2004 | 4 | 株式会社テスト 入社 |
| 2006 | 3 | 株式会社テスト 退社 |
| 2006 | 4 | 株式会社サンプル |
| | | 現在に至る |
| | | |
| | | |
| | | |
| | | |
| | | |
| | | 以上 |

| 年 | 月 | 学 歴 ・ 職 歴 （各別にまとめて書く） Education and Work History |
|---|---|---|
|  |  |  |
|  |  |  |
|  |  |  |
|  |  |  |
|  |  |  |
|  |  |  |
|  |  |  |

| 年 | 月 | 免 許 ・ 資 格 Skills & Certifications |
|---|---|---|
| 2020 | 1 | JLPT N1試験合格 |
|  |  |  |
|  |  |  |
|  |  |  |
|  |  |  |
|  |  |  |

| 特技、自己PRなど Self Introduction | 通勤時間 Commute Time |
|---|---|
| 2020年1月に日本語N1試験に合格しており、業務上のコミュニケーションにおいて日本語は問題ございません。 | 約　時間 55　分 |
|  | 扶養家族（配偶者を除く）Dependents<br>2 人 |
|  | 配偶者 Spouse　／　配偶者の扶養義務 Support<br>（有）・ 無　　　　有 ・（無） |

| 本人希望記入欄（特に給料・職種・勤務時間・勤務地・その他についての希望などがあれば記入）Personal Wishes |
|---|
| 営業職を希望します。勤務地、待遇などは貴社の規定に従います。 |

**The Shokumukeirekisho**

The Shokumukeirekisho, on the other hand, is a more detailed type of Japanese resume that's commonly used for full-time job applications. It's a structured document that provides a comprehensive overview of the applicant's education, work experience, and skills. This type of resume is usually printed, and the format is standardized. Unlike Western resumes, a Shokumukeirekisho focuses on an individual's work history and experience, rather than their skills and qualifications. In this guide, we will go through step by step on how to write a Shokumukeirekisho Japanese CV.

**Step 1: Personal Information**

The first step is to provide your personal information, including your full name, address, phone number, and email address. It is important to make sure that this information is accurate and up-to-date.

**Step 2: Career Summary**

The following step is to submit a brief career overview highlighting your professional experience. This should contain your job title, the name of the firm for which you worked, and the dates you worked there. It is also a good idea to note any significant milestones or achievements you had while in the job.

**Step 3: Work History**

The bulk of a Shokumukeirekisho consists of detailed information about your work history. This should include the name of the company you worked for, the dates of your employment, your job title, and a detailed description of your responsibilities and accomplishments in the role. It is important to be as specific as possible and to use measurable metrics whenever possible.

**Step 4: Education**

You should provide information about your schooling after your employment history. This should contain the names of the colleges you attended, as well as the dates you went and the degrees or certificates you received. You could also include any academic achievements or awards you have won.

**Step 5: Skills and Certifications**

Lastly, include a list of your abilities and credentials. This should contain any technical or professional talents you possess, as well as any certificates or licenses you hold. It is critical to be specific and list just talents relevant to the job you are looking for.

# Resume #2 — The Shokumukeirekisho (職務経歴書)

職務経歴書

基本情報
氏名
　山田 太郎
生年月日
　1990年1月1日
住所
　〒100-0000 東京都千代田区○○○○
電話番号
　090-1234-5678
メールアドレス
　taro.yamada@example.com

導入部
　ソフトウェア エンジニアは、新しいシステムの作成を担当しました。 資格と能力
については、基礎情報技術者試験に合格し、TOEIC 800 点を達成しています。

技術的スキルまたは資格
　8年間のJava開発経験

学歴
大学
　○○大学　工学部　情報工学科　卒業（20XX年3月）

職務経歴
　株式会社○○　　（20XX年4月〜現在）
　ソフトウェアエンジニア
　- Webアプリケーションの開発・保守
　- プロジェクト全体の進捗管理
　- 技術選定、アーキテクチャ設計
　- チームメンバーの育成

株式会社○○　　（20XX年1月〜20XX年3月）
　ソフトウェアエンジニア
　- 新規システムの開発
　- 開発環境の構築
　- 技術選定、アーキテクチャ設計

資格・スキル
　- 基本情報技術者試験 合格
　- TOEIC 800点

Shokumukeirekisho (職務経歴書) - The English Translation

Basic Information
Name
  Taro Yamada
Date of Birth
  January 1, 1990
Address
  〒100-0000 Chiyoda-ku, Tokyo, Japan
Phone Number
  090-1234-5678
Email
  taro.yamada@example.com

Introduction
  As a software engineer, I was responsible for creating a new system. Regarding his
  qualifications and abilities, he has passed the Basic Information Engineer Examination and
  has achieved a TOEIC score of 800.

Technical skills or qualifications
  8 years Java development experience

Education
University
  Bachelor of Engineering in Information Engineering, University of XX, March 20XX

Work Experience
  Company XX (April 20XX - Present)
  Software Engineer
  - Developed and maintained web applications
  - Managed project progress
  - Conducted technology selection and architecture design
  - Coached team members

  Company YY (January 20XX - March 20XX)
  Software Engineer
  - Developed a new system
  - Set up the development environment
  - Conducted technology selection and architecture design

Certificates and Skills
  - Passed the Basic Information Technology Engineer Examination
  - TOEIC score: 800

**Tips for Writing a Cover Letter**

When applying for a position, you must include a cover letter with your resume. In Japan, a cover letter is an essential part of the application process because it allows you to display your skills, qualifications, and experience to a potential employer. Writing a tailored cover letter that is specific to the job and company you are looking for can significantly increase your chances of being hired. Here are some tips for writing a job-winning resume letter for your job search in Japan.

**Research the Company**

Before you start writing your cover letter, research the company you are applying to. This will help you understand their values, mission, and goals. You can then tailor your cover letter to highlight how you are a good fit for the company and its culture.

**Address the Hiring Manager**

In Japan, it is essential to address the hiring manager by their name. Avoid using generic salutations like "To Whom It May Concern." Instead, take the time to research the name of the hiring manager and address them directly.

**Begin with a powerful introduction.**

The first line of your cover letter should be a powerful introduction that catches the recruiting manager's attention. Begin by describing the position you're looking for and how you heard about it.

**Emphasize Your Skills**

Highlight your credentials and expertise in the body of your cover letter. Use particular examples to demonstrate how your abilities and expertise are applicable to the position you're applying for. Make a point of mentioning any pertinent certifications or honors you've earned.

## Demonstrate Your Knowledge of the Company

In addition to highlighting your qualifications, demonstrate your knowledge of the company in your cover letter. Mention specific projects or initiatives that the company has undertaken and how you can contribute to their success.

**Finish with a powerful conclusion.**

Summarize why you are the best applicant for the position in the
concluding paragraph of your cover letter. Express your excitement for
the chance and express gratitude to the recruiting manager for their time
and thought.

**Editing and proofreading**

Proofread and revise your cover letter thoroughly before sending it.
Check for grammar and typographical mistakes. Request that a buddy
or mentor examine it for you in order to gain a new viewpoint.

**Common Mistakes To Avoid And Formatting Tips**

When it comes to applying for jobs in Japan, it's crucial to have a well-written resume and cover letter that follow the standard formats and conventions. Here are some typical mistakes to prevent, as well as some pointers to help you develop a winning application.

**Mistakes to Avoid**

1. Including Personal Information That Is Not Relevant to the Job

In Japan, it's common to include personal information such as your age, gender, and even a photograph on your resume. However, this information is not always relevant to the job and can lead to discrimination. Unless it's required by the employer, it's best to leave out personal information that is not necessary.

2. Using Informal Language

Japanese resumes and cover letters should be written in formal language. Avoid using colloquialisms, slang, or casual expressions. Instead, use polite and respectful language that reflects your professionalism.

3. Not Tailoring Your Application to the Job

Employers in Japan expect resumes and cover letters to be tailored to the specific job and company. Avoid sending generic applications that lack specific details about the job you're applying for. Instead, research the company and job requirements and customize your application accordingly.

4. Failing to Highlight Achievements and Skills

Japanese employers value candidates who can demonstrate their achievements and skills. Make sure to highlight specific examples of your accomplishments and the skills you have developed throughout your career.

**Formatting Tips**

1. Use a Standard Resume Format

Japanese resumes typically follow a standard format that includes your name and contact information, a professional summary, work experience, education, and skills. Make sure to use a standard format that is easy to read and understand.

2. Keep It Simple and Easy to Read

Japanese resumes and cover letters should be simple and easy to read. Avoid using fancy fonts or elaborate designs that can make your application difficult to read. Stick to a simple and professional format that showcases your skills and achievements.

3. Pay Attention to Details

Japanese employers are known for their attention to detail. Ensure your application is free of errors, typos, or grammatical mistakes. Use proper punctuation and capitalization, and double-check everything before submitting your application.

# Chapter Five

## Navigating the Job Search Process in Japan

Japan is recognized for its distinct culture and customs, which extends to the country's hiring procedure. Understanding the complexities of this procedure as a job seeker in Japan is critical when it comes to receiving a job offer with a respected firm. I recently got the opportunity to interview a recruiter in Japan to learn more about how recruiting works in Japan and how firms see hiring. The following are some major points from our discussion.

## Recruitment Process in Japan

The recruitment process in Japan is quite different from what you may be familiar with in other countries. Job seekers in Japan typically apply for jobs during a specific timeframe, which is usually in the spring of their final year of university or graduate school. This is known as the "shukatsu" period, which roughly translates to "job-hunting season." During this time, job seekers attend job fairs, company information sessions, and interviews in hopes of securing a job offer.

The shukatsu phase is unique to the Japanese recruiting procedure. Unlike in other countries, where job searchers can apply at any time of year, Japan's hiring procedure is strictly regulated and follows a precise calendar. This is because many Japanese firms hire a significant number of new graduates and hence must recruit on a massive scale.

Firms can streamline and improve their hiring operations during the shukatsu stage.

In Japan, the hiring process is also quite competitive, with numerous job seekers competing for a limited number of available positions. As a result, job seekers in Japan usually dedicate substantial time and effort to pre-interview preparation and business research. Attending job fairs and corporate information sessions, as well as completing internet research to discover more about the company's culture, values, and goals, are all part of this process.

Companies in Japan typically follow a structured recruitment process that involves multiple rounds of interviews. The first round is usually a group interview, where several candidates are interviewed at the same time. This is followed by a series of individual interviews with various members of the company, including HR personnel and department managers. In some cases, job seekers may also be required to take written tests or complete other tasks as part of the recruitment process.

**How Companies View Hiring**

In Japan, hiring is viewed as a long-term investment in an employee's career. Companies in Japan typically hire employees with the expectation that they will stay with the company for the long haul. As a result, companies in Japan strongly emphasize hiring candidates who are a good fit for the company's culture and values.

One way that companies in Japan assess whether a candidate is a good fit is through the use of group interviews. Group interviews are a common part of the recruitment process in Japan and are used to gauge a candidate's communication skills, teamwork abilities, and overall personality. During a group interview, candidates are asked to work together to solve a problem or complete a task, while being observed by members of the company.

Another key factor that companies in Japan consider when hiring is the candidate's educational background. In Japan, where education is highly valued, candidates who have attended prestigious universities or graduate schools are often viewed more favorably. Candidates who have not attended prestigious schools cannot be successful in their job search, but rather that education is highly prioritized in Japan.

Lastly, firms in Japan place a great premium on "soft skills" like as communication, teamwork, and flexibility. These abilities are seen as equally vital as technical abilities, and employers frequently seek people with a diverse range of talents and experiences. This is because organizations in Japan prioritize people who can work well with others and adapt to changing conditions, since these qualities are critical for long-term success within the company.

**Research and Preparation**

It is critical to conduct a study and prepare before beginning your job search in Japan. The first step is to determine the sort of work you want and the firms that provide it. To discover possible employers, you can utilize job search websites, recruiting firms, and professional networks.

Understanding the application process is another critical component of job hunting in Japan. Most employers expect a detailed CV and cover letter. It is critical that you adapt your application to the specific job and company to which you are applying.

It is also worth noting that some Japanese employers may need handwritten resumes from candidates. This may appear to be outdated, yet it is a regular practice in Japan. If you are unsure about your handwriting, you should practice before submitting your application.

**Job Hunting Culture**

In Japan, job hunting is a formal and structured process. The job hunting season usually starts in the fall, and most companies have a specific timeline for their recruitment process. Students frequently visit job fairs and corporate seminars to learn more about possible companies and employment prospects.

One unique aspect of job hunting in Japan is the emphasis on group interviews and assessments. Companies often invite multiple candidates to attend interviews and reviews together. This approach allows companies to evaluate individual skills, teamwork, and communication

abilities.

**Application Process**

As mentioned earlier, the application process in Japan is formal and requires a detailed resume and cover letter. It is critical to adapt your application to the exact job and organization for which you are applying. In Japan, it is common for companies to ask for a photograph of the applicant to be included in the application. This is not a discriminatory practice, but rather a way for companies to remember who they have interviewed.

It is also worth noting that some Japanese employers need handwritten resumes from candidates. This may seem outdated, but it is a common practice in Japan. If you are not confident in your handwriting, you may want to consider practicing before submitting your application.

**Job Hunting Season**

In Japan, the job hunting season typically starts in the fall, with most companies having specific recruitment timelines. It is important to know the recruitment timeline of the companies you are interested in, as they may be hiring at a different time than you are looking for a job.

Another important aspect of the job hunting season in Japan is attending job fairs and company seminars. These events are an opportunity to learn more about potential employers and job opportunities. Attending as many events as possible is recommended, as they can provide valuable information and connections.

**Cultural Differences**

While looking for work in Japan, it is critical to grasp the cultural differences. For example, the Japanese value humility and modesty, so it is important to avoid boasting about your accomplishments during interviews. Additionally, it is common to exchange business cards during interviews, so make sure to bring a sufficient amount with you.

Another cultural difference to be aware of is the importance of group harmony in Japanese companies. This is why many companies emphasize group interviews and assessments. It is important to demonstrate your ability to work well in a team during these assessments.

**How to Find Job Openings**

**Finding Job Opportunities through Recruitment Agencies in Japan**

Japan has good job opportunities for both natives and foreigners. Yet, getting a job in Japan may take a lot of work, especially for foreigners unfamiliar with the Japanese labor market. Recruitment companies may be of tremendous assistance in obtaining work in Japan. In this section, we will explore the major Japanese recruiting agencies, their distinctions, and how to communicate with them. We will also go through the benefits and drawbacks of utilizing Japanese staffing agencies.

## Major Recruitment Agencies in Japan

There are many recruitment agencies in Japan; below is a brief list of some of the major ones are the following.


- **Robert Walters**

- **Hays**

- **Michael Page**

- **Randstad**

- **Adecco**

- **Recruit Holdings**

- **Pasona Group**


Each of these agencies has its own strengths and weaknesses. Some specialize in certain industries, while others cater to a wide range of industries. Some have a large network of clients, while others focus on

providing personalized services to clients.


**Differences between Recruitment Agencies**


Recruitment agencies differ in several aspects, such as:


- Industry specialization

- Size of the agency

- Type of job opportunities offered

- Geographic location of clients and job seekers

- Level of personalized service


It is important to research and evaluate each agency based on your

needs and preferences before choosing one to work with to help you find employment. It is advantageous to live in Japan and hold a valid visa.

**Tips on Interacting with Recruitment Agencies**

While dealing with Japanese recruiting firms, keep the following suggestions in mind:

- Be professional: Dress appropriately and be polite in all your interactions with the agency.

- Be clear about your goals and expectations: Clearly communicate your career goals, job preferences, and expectations to the agency.

- Keep your resume up to date: Ensure that your resume is up to date and tailored to suit the job opportunities you are interested in.

- Follow up regularly: Follow up with the agency regularly to stay up to date on job opportunities and show your interest in finding a job.

**Benefits and Drawbacks of Using Recruitment Agencies in Japan**

Using recruitment agencies in Japan has its benefits and drawbacks. Some of the benefits include:

- Access to job opportunities: Recruitment agencies have access to a wide range of job opportunities that you might not otherwise know about.

- Industry expertise: Some recruitment agencies specialize in certain industries and have a wealth of knowledge about the industry and job market.

- Personalized service: Some recruitment agencies provide personalized services that can help you find job opportunities that match your skills and preferences.

**Drawbacks to Employing Recruiting Firms**

- Cost: Some recruitment agencies charge a fee for their services, which can be expensive.

- Limited job opportunities: Some recruitment agencies have a limited pool of job opportunities that might not match your skills or preferences.

- Lack of transparency: Some recruitment agencies might not be transparent about the job opportunities they offer and the companies they work with.

Recruitment agencies can be a great help in finding job opportunities in Japan. However, it is important to research and evaluates each agency based on your needs and preferences before choosing one to work with. Keep in mind the tips on interacting with agencies and weigh the benefits and drawbacks before making a decision.

**Online Job Hunting Resources in Japan**

If you are looking for a job in Japan, online job hunting resources can be a great way to explore job opportunities and find the right job for you. Japan has a wide range of online job hunting resources available to job seekers, including job sites, job boards, and recruitment agencies. In this section, we will discuss some of the most popular job sites in Japan, the types of jobs they offer, who should use them, how much they cost, and other tips to help you land your dream job.

## Who Should Use Them

Employment boards in Japan cater to both Japanese and foreign job searchers. However, certain employment sites, such as GaijinPot, cater primarily to international job searchers. It is critical to conduct research on the job posting before applying to verify that it is a good fit for you. If you are a foreigner searching for work in Japan, it may be beneficial to visit employment sites built exclusively for foreign job searchers, since they may provide extra tools and information to assist you negotiate the Japanese labor market.

## How Much They Cost

For job hunters, most employment sites in Japan are free to use. Nevertheless, some job boards may charge a fee for premium services such as job matching. When utilizing any employment site, check the terms and conditions to verify that you understand any fees or charges

that may apply.

**List of Job Sites**

## 1. GaijinPot

GaijinPot is a prominent job portal for foreign job searchers in Japan.

They provide a diverse range of employment, including education,

information technology, engineering, and hospitality. GaijinPot also

offers important information about living and working in Japan, such as

how to find accommodation, navigate the healthcare system, and obtain

a Japanese driver's license. If you are a foreigner seeking for work in

Japan, GaijinPot might be a fantastic place to start.

## 2. Daijob

Daijob is another popular job site in Japan that caters to both Japanese and foreign job seekers. They offer jobs in various industries such as IT, engineering, finance, and marketing. Daijob also provides useful information on visa requirements and living in Japan, including tips on how to obtain a work visa, find affordable housing, and navigate the Japanese healthcare system. If you are looking for a job in Japan and want a resource that caters to both Japanese and foreign job seekers, Daijob is a great place to start.

## 3. CareerCross

CareerCross is a job site that caters to bilingual job seekers in Japan. They offer jobs in various industries, including finance, IT, engineering, and hospitality. CareerCross also provides useful information on visa requirements and living in Japan, including tips on how to obtain a work visa and find affordable housing. If you are bilingual and looking for a job in Japan, CareerCross can be a great resource to help you find job opportunities that match your language skills.

## 4. LinkedIn

LinkedIn can help you connect with potential employers and build your professional network if you're searching for job in Japan. It is a platform that allows job seekers to create a professional profile, promote their skills and knowledge, and look for employment opportunities in their field of interest. Here are some tips on how to use LinkedIn effectively for job searching in Japan:

## 1. Create a Complete and Professional Profile

When utilizing LinkedIn for job searching in Japan, make sure your profile is thorough and professional. A high-quality profile photo, a well-written summary, and relevant professional experience and education are all required. A professional profile may help you stand out from the crowd and create a good first impression on prospective employers. You should also constantly update your profile to reflect any new skills, experiences, or accomplishments.

## 2. Join Relevant Groups

Joining relevant groups on LinkedIn can help you connect with professionals in your industry and stay up-to-date on industry news and trends. This can also help you find job openings that may not be posted elsewhere. You can search for groups by industry, location or interest, and join those that are most relevant to your career goals. You can also participate in group discussions and share your insights and knowledge to establish yourself as a thought leader in your field.

## 3. Use Keywords in Your Profile and Job Search

Use relevant terms in your profile and job search to appear in search results for possible employers. This is especially true in Japan, where many businesses utilize online search engines to discover applicants. Include keywords that are pertinent to your talents, experience, and the position you are seeking. You may also use LinkedIn's job search function to identify job vacancies that are a good fit for your skills and interests.

## 4. Research Companies and Connect with Recruiters

Using LinkedIn to research firms of interest and connect with recruiters is a terrific method to remain up to date on job vacancies and hiring procedures. Many employers use LinkedIn to locate possible applicants, so make sure your profile is current and professional. You may also use LinkedIn to learn more about the company's culture, beliefs, and mission to see whether it's a suitable fit for you. After that, you can contact recruiters or hiring managers to express your interest and learn more about the organization.

**Relevant Examples**

Here are some examples of how LinkedIn can be used for job hunting in Japan:

**Example 1: Finding a Job in the Tech Industry**

If you are looking for a job in the tech industry in Japan, you can use LinkedIn to connect with professionals in your industry and join relevant groups. You can also search for job openings using relevant keywords and connect with recruiters at companies that interest you. You can showcase your skills and experience by posting articles or sharing updates related to the latest trends in technology.

**Example 2: Finding a Job in the Hospitality Industry**

If you are looking for a job in the hospitality industry in Japan, you can use LinkedIn to research companies and connect with recruiters. You can also join relevant groups to stay up-to-date on industry news and connect with other professionals in your field. You can showcase your customer service skills and experience by sharing your insights on how to create memorable experiences for guests.

Overall, LinkedIn is an excellent tool for job hunting in Japan. By creating a complete and professional profile, joining relevant groups, using keywords in your profile and job search, and researching companies and connecting with recruiters, you can increase your chances of finding the right job for you. Remember to use LinkedIn consistently and strategically to build your brand and expand your network.

# 5. JET English Teaching Program

The JET (Japan Exchange and Teaching) Program provides a once-in-a-lifetime chance for young people from all around the world to visit Japan and learn about its culture while also earning significant teaching experience. The program is a Japanese government-sponsored effort aimed at encouraging local internationalization by bringing young people from all over the world together for exchange and foreign language instruction.

The JET Program offers a fantastic opportunity to experience Japan's culture, traditions, and language while working as an Assistant Language Teacher (ALT) or Coordinator for International Relations (CIR). Participants are placed in schools or local governments in Japan, where they can help teach English and other foreign languages to students.

**How to Apply**

Applications for the JET Program are open once a year, typically from October to November. The application process involves submitting an online application form, which includes a statement of purpose, a medical certificate, and your academic transcripts. You will also need to submit two letters of recommendation.

You must be a native English speaker with a Bachelor's degree or above to be eligible for the program. You should also be passionate about Japan and its culture. Please visit this website, https://jetprogramme.org/en/, for more information.

**Interview Process**

You will be invited to an interview if your application is successful. A panel of Japanese and English-speaking interviewers generally conducts the interview. The interview will put your Japanese knowledge, teaching ability, and communication skills to the test.

You should prepare for the interview by researching Japan's culture, customs, and traditions. You should also prepare to discuss your teaching philosophy and experience. Practice your communication skills, including speaking clearly and confidently.

**Tips for Applicants**

Here are some tips for applicants that can help them prepare for the

application process and interviews.


- Start researching Japan and its culture early on so that you can

  demonstrate your knowledge during the interview.


- Make sure that you have all the required documents ready

  before the application deadline. This includes your statement of

  purpose, medical certificate, and academic transcripts.

- Choose your recommenders carefully and make sure that they

  can speak to your teaching ability and cultural sensitivity.

- Practice your communication skills in advance, including your

  Japanese language skills if possible.


**More Information**

The JET Program offers a competitive salary and benefits package, including paid holidays, health insurance, and a relocation allowance. Participants are also given the opportunity to participate in various cultural activities and events.

If you are interested in the JET Program, be sure to visit the official JET Program website for more information. The website provides detailed information on the application process, interview tips, and life in Japan as a JET participant.

**6. Interac**

Interac is a recruitment agency that specializes in placing English teachers in Japanese schools. It offers training and support for its teachers and provides assistance with visa applications and relocation. This is the website of Interac https://www.interacnetwork.com/.

## Boston Career Forum: Tips for Job Hunting in Japan

The Boston Career Forum is the world's largest job fair for Japanese-English bilinguals. It is held annually in Boston and attracts thousands of participants looking to find work in Japan. Attending the Boston Career Forum can be an excellent opportunity to find work in Japan or with Japanese companies. It may, however, be a daunting experience, especially if you are new to the job search process or are unfamiliar with Japanese culture.

If you are interested in attending the Boston Career Forum or are currently job hunting in Japan, here are some tips to help you navigate the process:

## Timeline

The Boston Career Forum is usually held in November, so it's a good idea to start preparing for the event in the summer or early fall. This will give you enough time to research companies, update your resume, and practice your interviewing skills. You should also make sure your passport is up to date and start looking for flights and hotel accommodations well in advance.

## Cost

Attending the Boston Career Forum can be expensive, especially if you need to travel to Boston. However, many companies will reimburse your travel expenses if you are invited for an interview. In addition, some companies may offer to cover your flight and hotel expenses if you are a strong candidate. To reduce costs, you can also share hotel accommodations with other job seekers or look for cheaper alternatives like Airbnb.

## Who Should Attend

The Boston Career Forum is primarily for Japanese-English bilinguals who are interested in working in Japan. However, there are also opportunities for non-Japanese speakers who are interested in working for Japanese companies or in industries such as IT, finance, and consulting. If you are a recent graduate or are looking to change careers, the Boston Career Forum can be a great way to explore different options and connect with recruiters from top companies.

**Tips**

Research companies in advance and prepare a list of the ones you are interested in. Many companies will have booths at the event where you can learn more about their culture and job opportunities. Researching companies in advance will help you prioritize your time and maximize your chances of finding a job that suits your skills and interests.

Update your resume and have it reviewed by a native speaker. Your resume is your first impression with recruiters, so it's important to make sure it is polished and error-free. Consider having a native English speaker evaluate your resume for grammar and clarity if you are not a native English speaker. The same is recommended for Japanese resumes as well.

Interviewing skills should be practiced with a friend or mentor. The Boston Job Forum is a terrific place to network and meet recruiters, but it can also be scary. To gain confidence and prepare for frequent interview questions, practice your interviewing skills with a friend or mentor.

Bring many copies of your resume and dress professionally. Candidates that are well-prepared and presentable will be sought after by recruiters. Dress properly and bring numerous copies of your CV, as well as, if applicable, a portfolio of your work.

Prepare to answer questions regarding your language ability as well as your motivation for working in Japan. Several organizations will value your language skills as a bilingual Japanese-English speaker. Prepare to discuss your language skills and how they might be used to various professions. You should also be able to express your motivation for working in Japan and what you want to gain from experience.

Attending the Boston Career Forum may be a difficult yet rewarding experience. You may make the most of this event and get the job of your dreams in Japan if you prepare correctly and have the appropriate mentality.

**Job Search Strategies and Tips for submitting your application**

**How Many Applications You Should Have A Day**

Apply for at least twenty to fifty jobs daily to increase your chances of getting an interview. Numbers really do matter in this case. Yet, to enhance your chances of success, adapt your application to each position. This entails carefully reading the job description and tailoring your CV and cover letter to showcase your relevant abilities and expertise. You may enhance your chances of being recognized by hiring managers and securing an interview by personalizing your application to each position.

**How Many Average Interviews per Company**

The number of interviews per company varies depending on the company's hiring process. However, it is common for companies to conduct at least two to three interviews before making a hiring decision. This means that you may need to attend multiple interviews before you are offered a job. It is important to be patient and persistent in your job search and to keep applying for job opportunities even if you have attended multiple interviews without success.

**Additional Tips**

- Tailor your application to each job to increase your chances of success.
- Research the company before applying to ensure that it is the right fit for you.
- Be patient and persistent in your job search. The average job search will take several months.
- Network with industry professionals to increase your chances of finding a job.

**Job Fairs and Events in Japan**

Japan is a prosperous country known for its innovative technology, advanced manufacturing, and bustling finance industry. It is also home to many multinational companies from various industries, making it a desirable destination for job seekers worldwide. With the help of job fairs and events, job seekers can conveniently connect with potential employers, learn about different industries, and acquire valuable information about the job market in Japan. Here are some of the top job fairs and events in Japan:

**Career Forum**

Career Forum is one of Japan's most well-attended job fairs, held twice a year, in spring and autumn. DISCO International organizes the fair, and it attracts hundreds of companies from different industries, such as

IT, finance, engineering, and consulting. The fair also features seminars and workshops on various topics related to job hunting in Japan. The entry fee for the fair is around 1,000 yen. This job fair is ideal for those who are looking for a full-time job, internship, or part-time job in Japan.

**Asean Career Fair**

Asean Career Fair is a job fair that targets job seekers from Southeast Asia who are interested in working in Japan. The fair is held once a year, usually in October, and it is organized by the ASEAN-Japan Centre. The fair attracts companies from various industries such as manufacturing, hospitality, and IT. The entry fee for the fair is free. This job fair is perfect for those who are searching for a job opportunity in Japan in a particular industry.

**Who Should Attend?**

Job fairs and events in Japan are available to everyone who wants to work in Japan. Whether you are a recent graduate, an established professional, or a foreign job seeker, these events offer an excellent opportunity to network with possible employers and learn about various sectors. Visiting a job fair may help job searchers learn more about what businesses look for in their workers and network with other job seekers.

**What Type of Companies Are At Job Fairs**

Job fairs and events in Japan attract companies from various industries such as finance, IT, manufacturing, healthcare, and tourism. These companies range from small startups to large multinational corporations. Job seekers can interact with recruiters, attend seminars and workshops, and gain valuable information about the job market in Japan. This exposure can help job seekers to learn more about the different industries and the opportunities available in Japan.

Attending job fairs and events in Japan is an excellent way to find job opportunities and gain valuable information about the job market in Japan. From Career Forum to Asean Career Fair, these events offer a unique opportunity to meet potential employers, explore different industries, and connect with like-minded job seekers. Job seekers should take advantage of these events to learn more about the Japanese business culture, and the job market and to network with other job seekers. By doing so, they can increase their chances of finding their dream job in Japan.

**Making Direct Applications to Companies In Japan**

Are you interested in working for a specific company in Japan? If so, you may want to consider making a direct application. By applying directly to the company, you can avoid the middleman, which can give you a competitive edge.

Here are some pointers to help you with the process of making direct applications to Japanese companies:

**Research the Company**

Before making a direct application, it is essential to research the company thoroughly. This will help you to understand the company's culture, values, and mission, which can be helpful when crafting your application. It will also help you to know what to expect when it comes to the company's hiring process.

You can research the company by visiting their website, reading their annual reports, and checking their social media profiles. You can also reach out to current or former employees to learn more about the company's culture and hiring process.

**Prepare Your Application Materials**

When applying directly to a company in Japan, you will need to prepare a cover letter and resume. These materials should be tailored to the company and the position you are applying for.

Your cover letter should showcase your job-related talents and expertise. You should also demonstrate that you have researched the firm and explain why you wish to work for them. Your resume should be position-specific and highlight your relevant experience and qualifications.

## Consider Language

If you do not speak Japanese fluently, you may consider this while making a direct application. Make sure your application materials are written in Japanese or have been professionally translated. This implies that you have made an effort to study the language and culture of the firm.

You can also take language classes or work with a language tutor to improve your Japanese language skills. This can help you to communicate more effectively during the interview process.

## Submit Your Application

Once you have prepared your application materials, you should submit them directly to the company. You can do this by email or through the company's online application system. Be sure to follow the company's instructions carefully and provide all of the requested information.

You should also double-check your application documents before submitting them to verify that they are free of flaws, such as typos and grammatical problems.

**Follow-Up**

After submitting your application, you may want to follow up with the company to ensure that they have received it. You can do this by email or phone. Remember that the hiring process in Japan can be lengthy, so it may take some time to hear back from the company.

If you haven't heard from the company in a few weeks, send a polite follow-up email inquiring about the status of your application. This might show the company that you're interested in the position and want to learn more about it.

Making a direct application to a Japanese firm might be an excellent approach to demonstrate your abilities and expertise. By following these suggestions, you can improve your chances of success and finding the job you've been seeking for. Best wishes with your application!

# Chapter Six

# Interviewing in Japan: Tips and Strategies

If you are planning to interview for a job in Japan, you must understand the cultural norms and expectations surrounding the interview process. The Japanese job interview process is highly formal and structured, and you can expect to be interviewed by a panel of company representatives, rather than just one individual.

To assess your talents and expertise, the interviewers will most likely ask behavioral and situational questions. Job interviews in Japan are often quite extensive, with a range of questions designed to examine a candidate's history, talents, and personality.

It is common for interviewers to ask about your personal background, such as your family and hobbies, as a way to get to know you better. They may also ask about your long-term career goals and how you can contribute to the company's success.

**What to Expect During a Japanese Job Interview**

It is essential to be prepared for a highly structured and formal process during a Japanese job interview. Typically, the interview takes place in a conference room, and you will be seated across from a panel of interviewers. The interviewers may wear formal business attire, and you should also dress conservatively.

The self-introduction is one of the most important components of a Japanese job interview. You may be requested to provide a self-introduction in Japanese, so brush up on your language abilities beforehand. Your self-introduction should be succinct while emphasizing your talents, abilities, and experience.

Throughout the interview, it is also critical to maintain appropriate posture and create eye contact with the interviewers. Japanese interviewers highly value nonverbal communication, so be aware of your body language.

**How to Prepare for an Interview**

Before your interview, research the company and its culture to get a better understanding of what they value in employees. You can start by looking at the company's website, social media platforms, and any articles or news releases about the company.

This information can help you personalize your replies to the demands of the organization and reflect your interest in the position. Prepare questions to ask the interviewers to demonstrate your interest in the company and the role.

It is also essential to arrive early for your interview, as punctuality is highly valued in Japanese culture. You should also bring several copies of your resume and any other relevant documents, such as certificates or diplomas.

In addition to preparing your responses to potential interview questions, you should also practice your nonverbal communication skills. Japanese interviewers pay close attention to body language, so it is essential to maintain proper posture, make eye contact, and avoid fidgeting or slouching during the interview.

**How to Address Common Interview Questions**

Here are some common interview questions you may encounter during a Japanese job interview:

1. "Why do you want to work for this company?"

This question is often asked to gauge your level of interest and motivation. Be specific about what you admire about the company and how your skills and experience align with their mission and values.

2. "What are your strengths and weaknesses?"

Highlight your strengths and how they can contribute to the company's success. When discussing your weaknesses, be honest but also explain how you're working to improve in those areas.

3. "How do you handle stress or difficult situations?"

Provide examples of times when you've successfully managed stress or challenging situations in a professional setting. Show that you have a positive attitude and can remain calm under pressure.

4. "What are your long-term career goals?"

Be honest about your aspirations and how you see yourself growing within the company. Demonstrate that you're committed to your career and are looking for a long-term opportunity.

It is essential to prepare thoughtful and well-crafted responses to these questions, as they can help demonstrate your qualifications and suitability for the position.

By understanding the expectations of a Japanese job interview, preparing thoroughly, and practicing your interview skills, you'll be better equipped to make a positive impression on your potential employer.

# Chapter Seven

# Negotiating Job Offers and Contracts

If you're reading this, you're presumably interested in working in Japan or have recently been hired there. Congratulations! Japan is a land of limitless options, and with the appropriate attitude, you may have a rewarding work experience. Nonetheless, the Japanese workplace is well-known for its distinct cultural and professional demands, which can be difficult for unfamiliar people. This book will help you manage your expectations, adjust to your new job and life in Japan, and make the most of your Japanese work experience.

**Negotiating Salary and Benefits in Japan**

Salary and benefit negotiations are a crucial aspect of the job search

process. It is a method of ensuring that you are adequately rewarded for

your talents, experience, and qualifications, as well as securing a

package that suits your requirements. Salary negotiations in Japan, on

the other hand, might be distinctive and necessitate a different strategy

than in other nations. These are some pointers to consider while

negotiating your pay and perks in Japan.

**The Japanese Approach to Salary Negotiations**

In Japan, salary negotiations are typically conducted after a job offer.

Companies usually have a set salary range for each position, so it is

crucial to research and understand the industry standard for your

desired position. The Japanese approach to salary negotiations is often indirect, and it is common for the employer to make the first offer. It is essential to be respectful and patient during the negotiation process, as rushing negotiations or being too aggressive can be viewed negatively.

In Japan, the negotiating process is frequently viewed as a means of establishing trust and a healthy connection between the employer and employee. As a result, it is critical to approach talks in a way that demonstrates your interest in the firm and devotion to your work. This may be accomplished by inquiring about the corporate culture, the position, and the team, as well as expressing thanks for the offer.

**How to Research Salary Information**

It is critical to investigate the industry benchmark for your chosen position before negotiating your wage. This will give you a better idea of what to expect and will assist you in negotiating reasonable

Compensation. Salary information may be obtained by searching internet job boards, speaking with recruiters or headhunters, and networking with individuals in your preferred sector. While negotiating pay, it is also vital to consider the company's size, location, and industry.

Another way to research salary information is to ask current or former employees of the company. This can give you an insider's perspective on the company's pay structure and what to expect during negotiations. However, it is important to approach this with caution, as you do not want to come across as unprofessional or disrespectful.

The website Glassdoor, https://www.glassdoor.com/member/home/index.htm, can be a great resource for additional research.

**Negotiating Salaries in Japan**

It's important to note that salaries in Japan are not always negotiable, especially for entry-level positions. However, for more senior positions, negotiation may be possible. It's also essential to understand cultural differences when negotiating salaries in Japan. Directly asking for a higher salary may be viewed as impolite, so it's crucial to approach the conversation tactfully.

Salaries in Japan vary widely depending on the industry, company size, and location. While the country may offer high-paying positions, it's essential to do your research and understand the specific factors that impact salaries in your desired field. With this knowledge, you'll be better equipped to navigate the job market and negotiate a fair salary. It's also important to consider the overall financial benefit, taking into account the cost of living in different locations in Japan.

Job seeking in Japan is a complicated process that involves much planning and study. If you intend to seek for work in Japan, it is critical that you grasp the country's job-hunting culture and conventions. This book will provide you an insight of the job search process in Japan.

**Tips for Negotiating Benefits**

In addition to salary, negotiating benefits is also an important part of the negotiation process. Benefits such as health insurance, vacation time, and retirement plans are common benefits offered by Japanese companies. When negotiating benefits, it is important to understand the company's policies and what benefits are negotiable. It is recommended to prioritize the benefits that are most important to you and be prepared to compromise on others.

When negotiating benefits, it is important to do so in a way that shows your understanding of the company's policies and your commitment to your role. This can be achieved by asking questions about the benefits package, expressing gratitude for the offer, and being prepared to compromise on certain benefits if necessary.

Overall, negotiating salary and benefits in Japan requires research, patience, and a respectful approach. By understanding the Japanese approach to negotiations and researching industry standards, you can negotiate a fair salary and benefits package for your desired position. Remember to approach negotiations as a way to build trust and establish a positive relationship with your employer, and to prioritize the benefits that are most important to you.

# Chapter Eight

# Adjusting to Work Culture in Japan

Japan is known for its unique work culture, which can be quite different from what many people are used to. Understanding and adapting to this culture is key to success in a Japanese workplace. Here are some unique aspects of Japanese work culture, as well as tips for adapting to the work environment and building relationships with colleagues.

## Unique Aspects of Japanese Work Culture

### Long Working Hours

In Japan, it is not uncommon for employees to work long hours, often well into the evening. This is seen as a sign of dedication and hard work and is expected of many employees. Overtime pay is often minimal or nonexistent, so it is important to be prepared for long hours. To manage long hours, you can take frequent breaks, prioritize your work, and communicate with your team to distribute the workload.

**Group Focus**

The Japanese work culture prioritizes the collective over the individual. As a result, choices are frequently reached by agreement, with everyone working toward a single objective. It is critical to be a team player and to put the demands of the group ahead of your own. To be an excellent team player, you must listen carefully to your colleagues, be receptive to feedback, and cooperate effectively.

**Hierarchy**

In both culture and business, Japan has a strong sense of hierarchy. Respect for individuals in positions of power is essential, as is deferring to their judgment. This implies that choices are frequently made by individuals in positions of power, and it is critical to accept this and not oppose authority. To show respect, acknowledge your superiors with appropriate honorifics, avoid interrupting them, and avoid publicly opposing them.

**Etiquette**

Etiquette and protocol are highly valued in Japanese workplace culture. Several standards must be followed, such as bowing while meeting someone, using honorific language to express respect, and exchanging business cards with both hands. It is critical to understand and adhere to these guidelines. To prevent making mistakes, watch how your colleagues respond, get guidance from your mentor, and practice until you feel secure.

**Adapting to the Work Environment**

**Learning the Language**

Learning Japanese is vital for employment success in Japan. Even if your coworkers speak English, it is crucial to demonstrate that you are attempting to learn the language and understand the culture. This will help you create relationships with your coworkers and demonstrate your dedication to your career. You may attend language lessons, practice with your coworkers, and learn about Japanese culture.

**Be Punctual**

The Japanese work culture places a high value on timeliness. It is critical to come on time and to be prepared to begin work at the allocated hour. Tardiness is interpreted as contempt and a lack of commitment. To avoid being late, schedule your commute ahead of time, set alarms or reminders, and organize your work materials ahead of time.

## Dress Appropriately

Japanese work culture places a strong emphasis on appearance. It is important to dress professionally and conservatively, with men wearing suits and ties and women wearing conservative business attire. It is also important to keep your appearance neat and tidy throughout the day. To dress appropriately, you can observe how your colleagues dress, ask for advice from your mentor, and invest in high-quality work clothes.

**Build Relationships**

Developing relationships with your coworkers is critical for success in a Japanese company. This entails getting to know your coworkers and demonstrating an interest in their life outside of work. Participating in social activities such as after-work drinks and corporate trips is also vital. Join clubs or groups to meet new people, inquire about your coworkers' hobbies or interests, and offer to assist them with their job.

**Tips for Building Relationships with Colleagues**

**Participate in Social Events**

Social events are an important part of Japanese work culture. It is important to participate in these events and get to know your colleagues outside of work. This can help you build relationships and establish trust with your colleagues. Some popular social events include nomikai, which are drinking parties, and enkai, which are company-wide parties.

## Show Interest in Your Colleagues

Showing interest in your colleagues is essential for building relationships in a Japanese workplace. This means asking about their lives outside of work, such as their hobbies and interests, and showing genuine interest in what they have to say. You can also offer to help them with their work or ask for their advice on a project.

## Use Honorific Language

Using honorific language is an important part of Japanese work culture. This means using respectful language when speaking to your colleagues, and addressing those in higher positions with appropriate honorifics. This can help show respect and build trust with your colleagues. You can learn honorific language by practicing with your colleagues, studying Japanese language textbooks, and observing how your colleagues speak.

**Be Patient**

Building relationships takes time, especially in a culture as group-focused as Japan. It is important to be patient and persistent and to continue to make efforts to build relationships with your colleagues over time. You can also ask your mentor for advice on how to build relationships and be open to feedback from your colleagues.

**Managing Expectations in the Japanese Workplace**

Communication in Japan is sometimes oblique, making it difficult to understand what is expected of you. To thrive in the Japanese workplace, pay close attention to nonverbal signs and ask clarifying questions as needed.

**Settling Into Your New Job and Life in Japan**

Relocating to a new country may be stressful, but there are actions you can do to make the move easier. Here are some ideas to help you adjust to your new job and lifestyle in Japan.

**Join Clubs or Groups**

Joining a club or group can be a great way to meet new people and build connections outside of work. Whether it's a sports team, a language exchange group, or a hobby club, finding a community of like-minded people can make your time in Japan more enjoyable. It's also a great way to practice your Japanese language skills and learn more about Japanese culture.

# Chapter Nine

# Embracing Your New Career in Japan

Congratulations on your new job in Japan! Starting a new career in a foreign country can be challenging, but also rewarding. Japan has a unique culture and work environment that is different from what you may have experienced in your home country. With the right mindset, attitude, and effort, you can make the most of your new job and succeed in your role.

**Making the Most of Your New Job**


**Be Open-minded and Flexible**


Japan has a unique and fascinating culture. Embrace the differences and be willing to adapt to new ways of doing things. Be open to learning new things and trying new experiences. Embracing the culture will help you adapt more easily and make deeper connections with your colleagues.


**Build Relationships**


In Japan, networking is very beneficial. Spend time getting to know your coworkers and developing connections with them. This will allow you to better grasp the corporate culture and work more efficiently.

People in Japan place a high emphasis on connections and are more inclined to do business with people they know and trust.

## Learn the Language

While it's not necessary to become fluent in Japanese, learning some basic phrases and vocabulary will help you communicate better with your coworkers and clients. Learning the language will also help you understand the culture and make deeper connections with your colleagues.

## Take Advantage of Training Opportunities

Many companies in Japan offer various training programs for employees. Attend these programs to improve your skills and knowledge. This will show your employer that you are dedicated to your job and eager to learn and grow professionally.

## Tips for Succeeding in Your Role

Make sure you understand exactly what is expected of you in your work. If necessary, ask questions and seek clarification. This will allow you to do your work more successfully and satisfy your boss's expectations.

## Be Proactive

Take initiative and look for ways to improve processes and procedures. This will show your employer that you are committed to your job and eager to contribute to the company's success. Being proactive will also help you stand out from your colleagues and be recognized for your efforts.

## Meet Deadlines

In Japan, punctuality is highly valued. Make sure to meet your deadlines and deliver quality work on time. This will demonstrate your reliability and professionalism to your employer.

## Communicate Effectively

Japanese communication style can be indirect. Be patient and listen carefully to what others are saying. Confirm your understanding by paraphrasing what you heard. This will help you avoid misunderstandings and build trust with your colleagues.

**Continuing Learning and Growing Professionally**

Look for classes, seminars, and workshops that can help you improve your skills and knowledge. This will enable you to stay up to date on the latest trends and breakthroughs in your field, making you a more valuable addition to your company.

**Find a Mentor**

A mentor can provide guidance and advice on navigating the Japanese business world. They can share their experiences and help you develop a plan for achieving your career goals.

**Keep Current On Industry News**

To remain up to date on trends and advancements in your sector, read industry magazines and attend industry events. This will assist you in remaining relevant and competitive in your field.

**Engage In Self-reflection**

Consider your performance and opportunities for improvement.

Establish and strive toward goals for yourself. This will assist you in

consistently improving and growing professionally.

# Chapter Ten

# Conclusion

If you are looking for a job in Japan, you might have encountered a lot of challenges such as language barrier, cultural differences, and unfamiliarity with the Japanese job market. However, reading this book should have given you a good understanding of the job hunting process in Japan, and hopefully, it has been helpful in your job search.

The book has covered various aspects of job hunting in Japan, including the job market, job search strategies, resumes and cover letters, interviews, and negotiations. By following the tips and advice provided in the book, you can increase your chances of landing a job that is a good fit for you.

**Final Thoughts**

Job hunting in Japan can be a daunting process, especially for foreigners. Nevertheless, with the right preparation and understanding of the process, you can overcome the challenges and succeed in your job hunt.

Being patient and persistent is one of the most important things to remember. The work market in Japan may be competitive, and finding the ideal position may take some time. Yet, if you remain focused and continue to apply, you will ultimately discover a job that suits your requirements.

Maintaining a pleasant attitude and being open to learn are also essential. It may take some time to adjust to Japanese work culture. But, if you approach the job search process with an open mind and a

willingness to learn, you will be able to adapt and succeed.

# Additional Resources

## Additional Recruitment Agencies in Japan

| Rank | Name of Agency | Industries Specialized | Number of Employees |
|---|---|---|---|
| 1 | Pasona Group | Business support, finance, IT, engineering, healthcare, hospitality, education, retail, and more | 7,000+ |
| 2 | en world | IT, finance, engineering, healthcare, hospitality, and more | 5,000+ |
| 3 | Robert Walters | Accounting, finance, banking, legal, HR, IT, sales, marketing, supply chain, and more | 1,000+ |
| 4 | Hays | Accounting, finance, banking, construction, engineering, IT, legal, HR, sales, marketing, and more | 1,000+ |

| 5 | Morgan McKinley | Accounting, finance, banking, engineering, IT, legal, HR, sales, marketing, and more | 500+ |
| 6 | Michael Page | Accounting, finance, banking, construction, engineering, IT, legal, HR, sales, marketing, and more | 500+ |
| 7 | JAC Recruitment | Accounting, finance, banking, legal, HR, IT, sales, marketing, and more | 500+ |
| 8 | RGF Professional | Accounting, finance, banking, engineering, IT, legal, HR, sales, marketing, and more | 500+ |
| 9 | Spring転職エージェント | Accounting, finance, banking, engineering, IT, legal, HR, sales, marketing, and more | 500+ |
| 10 | JAC International | Accounting, finance, banking, legal, HR, IT, sales, marketing, and more | 500+ |

| 11 | RGF HR Agent | Accounting, finance, banking, engineering, IT, legal, HR, sales, marketing, and more | 500+ |
| 12 | ManpowerGroup | Accounting, finance, banking, engineering, IT, legal, HR, sales, marketing, and more | 500+ |
| 13 | Link Japan Careers | IT, finance, engineering, healthcare, hospitality, and more | 50-100 |
| 14 | East West Consulting | IT, finance, engineering, healthcare, hospitality, and more | 50-100 |
| 15 | Robert Half | Accounting, finance, banking, legal, HR, IT, sales, marketing, and more | 50-100 |

**The S.T.A.R. Interview Format**

The S.T.A.R. interview format is a commonly used method for answering interview questions that assess a candidate's behavioral competencies. The acronym S.T.A.R. stands for Situation, Task, Action, and Result. This format is designed to help the candidate provide a structured and detailed response to a behavioral interview question.

**Situation**

The first component of the S.T.A.R. format is the Situation. This is where the candidate sets the stage by describing the specific situation that they faced. The candidate should provide enough context and detail to help the interviewer understand the circumstances surrounding the situation. The Situation component is crucial because it helps the interviewer evaluate the candidate's ability to identify and define problems accurately.

**Task**

In the Task component of the S.T.A.R. format, the candidate outlines the aim or goal that they were aiming to achieve in the situation. This enables the interviewer to have a better understanding of what the candidate was seeking to accomplish. The Task component is important because it allows the interviewer to evaluate the candidate's ability to create goals and priorities that are consistent with the organization's objectives.

## Action

The Action component of the S.T.A.R. format is where the candidate describes the specific actions they took to address the situation and achieve their objective. This is where the candidate can highlight their skills, abilities, and decision-making process. The Action component is critical because it helps the interviewer evaluate the candidate's ability to take action and make decisions under challenging circumstances.

## Result

The Outcome is the last component of the S.T.A.R. format. This is the section in which the candidate discusses the consequence of their activity. Where feasible, they should be explicit and quantifiable. The interviewer will seek proof of the candidate's effect and contribution. The Result component is important since it allows the interviewer to evaluate the candidate's ability to achieve outcomes and satisfy

objectives.

**Example**

Here's a S.T.A.R. solution to the question, "Tell me about a time when you had to work with a difficult team member."

Situation: On a project for our customer, I was on a team with a colleague who had a reputation for being tough to deal with.

Task: My objective was to ensure that we completed the project on time and to the client's satisfaction.

Action: I scheduled a one-on-one meeting with my colleague to discuss his concerns and how we could work together effectively. I listened actively and tried to understand his perspective. I also shared my concerns and suggestions for how we could improve our collaboration.

We agreed on a plan of action, and I made regular check-ins to ensure we were both on track.

Result: As a result of our improved collaboration, we completed the project on time and to the client's satisfaction. My colleague and I built a more positive working relationship, which improved our ability to work together on future projects.

Using the S.T.A.R. format can help candidates provide clear, concise, and detailed responses to behavioral interview questions, which can help them stand out in the job market. By using this method, candidates can demonstrate their problem-solving skills, goal orientation, decision-making abilities, and track record of delivering results.

In summary, the S.T.A.R. interview format provides employers with a standardized method of evaluating candidates' behavior competencies.

It is a valuable tool in assessing candidates' suitability for a particular

role, and it can help candidates showcase their skills, abilities, and

accomplishments in a structured and effective manner.

**20 Tips for Job Hunting in Japan**

Job hunting in Japan can be overwhelming, especially for foreigners unfamiliar with the culture and customs. The following are 20 tips to help you navigate the job market in Japan.

1. Research the company thoroughly before applying. In Japan, companies expect applicants to deeply understand their business and values. If you're applying to a Japanese company, it's essential to research the company's history, mission, values, and culture to get a better understanding of what they're looking for in a candidate. You can explore the company's website, social media, and news articles to gather information about the company.

2. Customize your resume to fit the job description. Japanese employers prefer resumes that are tailored to the specific job opening. Ensure your

resume highlights your relevant skills and experiences that match the job requirements. Also, use keywords from the job posting to show that you understand the position's requirements.

3. Use a professional photo on your resume. In Japan, appearance is essential; a professional headshot can make a good impression. Make sure your photo is a high-quality headshot showing you in professional attire and a friendly smile.

4. Learn Japanese. While some companies may have English as their official language, knowing Japanese will give you a significant advantage in the job market. Knowing the language will help you communicate effectively with your colleagues and clients, and it will also help you understand the culture and customs of Japan.

5. Network, network, network. In Japan, personal connections are

crucial to finding a job. Attend job fairs and industry events to meet people in your field. Joining professional organizations is also a great way to expand your network and learn about job opportunities.

6. Be prepared for multiple rounds of interviews. Japanese companies often have a rigorous interview process that can include several rounds of interviews and assessments. Be sure to prepare thoroughly for each round and be patient.

7. Dress appropriately for interviews. In Japan, conservative business attire is expected for job interviews. Men should wear a dark suit and tie, and women should wear a conservative dress or suit.

8. Be on time. Punctuality is highly valued in Japan, and even a few minutes late can leave a negative impression. Ensure you arrive at least 10-15 minutes before your scheduled interview time.

9. Bring a copy of your resume in Japanese. Even if the company doesn't require it, having a Japanese version of your resume can show your commitment to the job. It also shows that you're willing to take the extra effort to communicate with your potential employers in their language.

10. Follow up with a thank-you note or email after the interview. This is a common practice in Japan and can help you stand out from other applicants. Be sure to express your appreciation for the opportunity to interview and reiterate your interest in the position.

11. Be patient. The job search process in Japan can take longer than in other countries, so don't get discouraged if you don't hear back right away. Keep applying to other jobs and stay positive.

12. Consider working with a recruiter. Many companies in Japan rely on recruiting agencies to find candidates, so working with a recruiter can increase your chances of finding a job. Recruiters can help you find job opportunities that match your skills and preferences.

13. Be aware of visa requirements. If you are a foreigner, make sure you understand the visa requirements before applying to a job in Japan. You may need to obtain a work visa before you can start working in Japan.

14. Be honest about your language abilities. Japanese companies value honesty, and exaggerating your language skills on your resume can backfire during the interview process. If you're not proficient in Japanese, it's better to be honest and show your willingness to learn.

15. Consider taking a language proficiency test. Having a certification

in Japanese language proficiency can make you more competitive in the job market. The Japanese Language Proficiency Test (JLPT) is a standardized test that measures Japanese language proficiency.

16. Understand the work culture. In Japan, the work culture is highly structured and hierarchical, and companies expect employees to adhere to strict standards of behavior and respect. Understanding the culture can help you adjust to your new workplace and build better working relationships.

17. Be open to learning new skills. Japanese companies value employees who are willing to learn and adapt to new challenges. Be open to new experiences and take advantage of training opportunities.

18. Show enthusiasm for the company and its culture. Japanese companies value employees who are passionate about their work and

committed to the company's goals. Research the company's culture and history and show your enthusiasm during the interview.

19. Be prepared for long working hours. In Japan, it is common to work long hours, and many companies expect employees to work overtime without additional pay. Make sure that you're prepared to handle the workload and work-life balance.

20. Have realistic expectations. While Japan offers many job opportunities, competition can be fierce, and it may take time to find the right job. Be patient and persistent in your job search, and don't give up on your career goals.

**50 Useful Japanese Work-Related Phrases for Job Hunting**

1. お疲れ様でした (Otsukaresama deshita) – Thank you for your hard work

This expression is frequently used to express gratitude and respect to coworkers or superiors after finishing a task or assignment.

2. 就職活動 (Shuushoku katsudou) – Job hunting

This phrase refers to the process of looking for a job, which can include attending job fairs, submitting resumes, and going to interviews.

3. 履歴書 (Rirekisho) – Resume

This is a document that summarizes a person's work experience, education, and other qualifications. It is often required when applying for a job in Japan.

## 4. 面接 (Mensetsu) – Interview

This refers to the process of meeting with a potential employer to discuss job qualifications, skills, and experience.

## 5. エントリーシート (Entoriishito) – Entry sheet

This is a form that companies often require applicants to fill out as part of the application process. It typically asks for personal information, education history, work experience, and other qualifications.

## 6. 面接対策 (Mensetsu taisaku) – Interview preparation

This refers to the process of getting ready for a job interview, which can include researching the company, practicing responses to common interview questions, and dressing appropriately.

## 7. 自己PR (Jikou PR) – Self-promotion

This refers to the practice of highlighting one's strengths and qualifications during a job interview or on an application.

## 8. 経験値 (Keikenchi) — Experience

This refers to a person's work or life experience, which can be an important factor in determining whether they are a good fit for a job.

## 9. スキル (Sukiru) — Skills

This refers to a person's abilities and talents, such as communication, leadership, or technical skills.

## 10. 業務経歴書 (Gyoumu keirekisho) — Work history document

This is a more detailed version of a resume that provides a comprehensive overview of a person's work experience and qualifications.

11. 職務経歴書 (Shokumu keirekisho) – Job history document

This is another type of work history document that focuses specifically on a person's job experience.

12. 応募資格 (Ouboshi-kaku) – Qualifications for applying

This refers to the requirements that a company may have for applicants, such as education level, work experience, or language skills.

13. 人材募集 (Jinzai boshuu) – Recruitment

This refers to the process of seeking out and attracting potential employees for a company.

14. 採用 (Saiyou) – Hiring

This refers to the process of selecting and offering a job to a candidate.

## 15. 選考 (Senkou) – Selection process

This refers to the process of reviewing applications, conducting

interviews, and making a final decision on who to hire.

## 16. 募集要項 (Boshuu youkou) – Recruitment

## requirements

This refers to the qualifications and requirements that a company may

have for applicants, which are typically listed in job postings or on the

company's website.

## 17. 給与 (Kyuujo) – Salary

This refers to the amount of money that an employee will be paid for

their work.

## 18. 福利厚生 (Fukuri kousei) – Benefits

This refers to the perks and benefits that an employee may receive as part of their job, such as health insurance, retirement savings plans, or paid time off.

## 19. 勤務時間 (Kinmu jikan) – Work hours

This refers to the hours that an employee is expected to work each day or week.

## 20. 休日 (Kyuujitsu) – Holidays

This refers to the days when an employee is not expected to work, such as weekends, national holidays, or vacation days.

## 21. 出勤 (Shukkin) – Attendance

This refers to the act of showing up to work on time and being present during work hours.

## 22. 退職 (Taisshoku) – Resignation

This refers to the act of voluntarily leaving a job.

## 23. 辞める (Yameru) – To quit

This is a more informal way of saying "resignation."

## 24. 退社 (Taissha) – Leaving the company

This is another way of saying "resignation."

## 25. 退職金 (Taisshokukin) – Severance pay

This refers to the money that an employee may receive upon leaving a job, which can be used to help them transition to a new job or career.

## 26. 残業 (Zangyou) – Overtime

This refers to the hours that an employee works beyond their regular work hours.

## 27. 仕事量 (Shigoto-ryou) – Workload

This refers to the amount of work that an employee is expected to complete within a certain period of time.

## 28. 責任 (Sekinin) – Responsibility

This refers to the duties and obligations that an employee has to their job, their colleagues, and their company.

## 29. 報告 (Houkoku) – Report

This refers to the act of providing information or updates on a project or task to a supervisor or colleague.

## 30. 承認 (Shounin) – Approval

This refers to the act of giving permission or granting approval for a task or project.

## 31. 支払い (Shiharai) – Payment

This refers to the act of paying for goods or services, or receiving

payment for work done.

## 32. 連絡先 (Renrakusaki) – Contact information

This refers to a person's phone number, email address, or other means

of communication that can be used to contact them.

## 33. 雇用契約 (Koyou keiyaku) – Employment contract

This is a legal agreement between an employee and an employer

outlining the terms and conditions of employment.

## 34. 労働基準法 (Roudou kijunhou) – Labor Standards

Act

In Japan, this is a system of legislation that controls employers' and employees' rights and obligations, including minimum pay, working hours, and other labor-related concerns.

## 35. 労働時間 (Roudou jikan) – Working hours

This refers to the hours that an employee is expected to work each day or week.

## 36. 安全衛生 (Anzen eisei) – Safety and health

This refers to the measures that a company takes to ensure the safety and well-being of its employees, such as providing protective equipment or training on workplace hazards.

## 37. 組織 (Soshiki) – Organization

This refers to the structure and hierarchy of a company, including its departments, teams, and management.

## 38. 社風 (Shafuu) – Corporate culture

This refers to the beliefs, attitudes, and norms that shape an organization's workers' conduct and relationships.

## 39. チームワーク (Chiimuwaaku) – Teamwork

This refers to the ability of employees to work together effectively to achieve common goals.

## 40. 挑戦 (Chousen) – Challenge

This refers to the opportunity to take on new and difficult tasks or projects that can help an employee grow and develop professionally.

## 41. 成果 (Seika) – Results

This refers to the outcomes or achievements that a person or company has accomplished as a result of their work.

## 42. 目標 (Mokuhyou) – Goals

This refers to the specific targets or objectives that a person or company is working to achieve.

## 43. 意欲 (Iyoku) – Motivation

This refers to a person's drive and enthusiasm for their work, which can help them overcome challenges and achieve success.

## 44. 達成感 (Tasseikan) – Sense of accomplishment

This refers to the feeling of satisfaction or pride that a person experiences after achieving a goal or completing a task.

## 45. 信頼 (Shinrai) – Trust

This refers to the confidence and reliability that colleagues and superiors have in a person's abilities and character.

## 46. コミュニケーション能力 (Komyunikeeshon nouryoku) – Communication skills

This refers to a person's capacity to successfully communicate with others, both vocally and in writing.

## 47. リーダーシップ (Riidaashippu) – Leadership

This refers to the ability to guide and motivate others to achieve common goals and objectives.

## 48. 創造性 (Souzousei) – Creativity

This refers to the capacity to generate fresh and inventive ideas, solutions, or goal achievement.

## 49. 柔軟性 (Juunan-sei) – Flexibility

This refers to the ability to adapt to changing circumstances, such as new tasks or responsibilities, or unexpected challenges.

## 50. ストレス管理 (Sutoresu kanri) – Stress management

This refers to the practices and techniques that a person can use to cope with stress and maintain their mental and emotional well-being in the workplace.

**Questions to Ask Employer During the Interview Process**

**First Interview - "The Screening Interview"**

(Likely with recuiter or company employee)

1. Can you please describe the company culture in Japan?

2. How do you measure success for this role?

3. What are the expectations for this position after 6 months?

4. Are there opportunities for advancement?

5. What has your experience been like working the company?

6. What qualities do successful employees at this company possess?

7. What are the next steps in the interview process and when can I expect to hear back?

**Second Interview - "The Fit Interview"**

(Likely with company executive or team member)

1. Could you please elaborate on the role's day-to-day responsibilities?

2. What are the biggest challenges in this role?

3. What challenges does the company currently face and how can this role contribute to addressing them?

4. Can you describe how this role interacts with others in the company?

5. Can you describe the team I will be working with?

6. Can you describe the communication channels within the team?

7. If I am successful today, what steps should I take to prepare for the next phase in the interview process?

**Third Interview - "The Senior Leadership Interview"**

(Likely with the company CEO or human resources manager)

1. What do you see as the biggest opportunities for growth within the company?

2. How does the company stay innovative and competitive in the industry?

3. What is the management style like at this company?

4. How does the company approach work-life balance and employee wellness?

5. How does the company support employee growth and development?

6. Can you describe the onboarding process for new hires?

7. Is there any additional information you need from me or anything else I can provide to demonstrate my fit for this role?

8. What is the next step and what is the timeline for making a hiring decision?

**Interview Questions For The Interviewee and Sample Answers**

1. Tell me about yourself.

   - Sample Answer: "I am a recent graduate with a degree in computer science. I have experience in coding and software development through internships and personal projects. I'm excited to apply my skills in a professional setting."

2. How much do you know about our firm? - Example Response: "I have looked into your company and discovered that you specialize in building mobile applications. I'm pleased by your creative approach to issue solving in the business, as well as your dedication to client happiness."

3. What are your strengths and weaknesses?

   - Sample Answer (Strengths): "I believe my strengths are my ability to work well under pressure, my attention to detail, and my strong communication skills."

- Sample Answer (Weaknesses): "I'm a bit of a perfectionist, which may occasionally stymie my growth. Yet, I am aware of this and am attempting to balance my need for excellence with the requirement for efficiency."

4. Why do you want to work for us?

   - Sample Answer: "I am eager to work for your company because I am passionate about developing software that solves real-world problems. I believe that your company's focus on innovation and customer satisfaction aligns with my own values."

5. Describe a time when you had to overcome a challenge.

   - Sample Answer: "With my previous internship, I was entrusted with creating an application in a short period of time. To keep on schedule, I needed to work swiftly and efficiently while still communicating effectively with my team. We were eventually able to provide a high-quality product on schedule."

6. What are your salary expectations?

- Sample Answer: "I am flexible in terms of salary and would like to discuss this further during the negotiation process."

7. What do you think makes you a good fit for this role?

- Sample Answer: "I feel that my technical abilities, attention to detail, and ability to work well in a team make me an excellent candidate for this role. I am also enthusiastic about the opportunity to learn and grow in this capacity."

8. How do you handle stress and pressure?

- Sample Answer: "I handle stress and pressure by prioritizing my tasks and focusing on the most important ones first. I also make sure to take breaks and practice self-care to avoid burnout."

9. What are your long-term career goals?

- Sample Answer: "My long-term professional ambition is to become a software development manager. I am enthusiastic about the opportunity to learn and grow in this capacity, and I feel it will help me reach my future professional objectives."

10. Do you have any questions for us?

   - Sample Answer: "Yes, I would like to know more about the company culture and opportunities for professional development within the organization."

# Tokyo Paul's Other Books

<table>
<tr><td>

**Title:**

Japan Info Guide: Tips & Photos For An Amazing Experience in Japan!

**Description:**

This book is your ticket to the most current, relevant recommendations on what to see and skip and what undiscovered gems are waiting for you. I share my years of experience traveling and living in Japan with you. With your dependable travel buddy, see more than a hundred temples in Kyoto, unwind in a hot spring strewn over the island, and savor the diversity of Japan's delicious foods. Start your tour immediately, enjoy my high-quality photos, and get to the heart of Japan with me.

</td><td>

**Book Cover:**

</td></tr>
</table>

## Tokyo Paul's Other Books

<table>
<tr><td>

**Title:**
Japan Photobook 2023

**Description:**
This wonderful Japan Photobook contains more than 75 pages of breathtaking images from my YouTube Japan travels. You can visit the same locations because they are well-marked! Discover the gorgeous towns and sites of Japan through breathtaking photographs. Let the stunning cityscapes, festival scenes, cherry blossoms, and illuminations take you there! This book includes images of excellent quality and resolution. Every city, including Akihabara, Asakusa, Yokohama, Ueno, Ginza, Hakone, Nikko, etc., has a breathtaking atmosphere. This fantastic book beautifully captures Japan's incredible energy and way of life.

</td><td>

**Book Cover:**

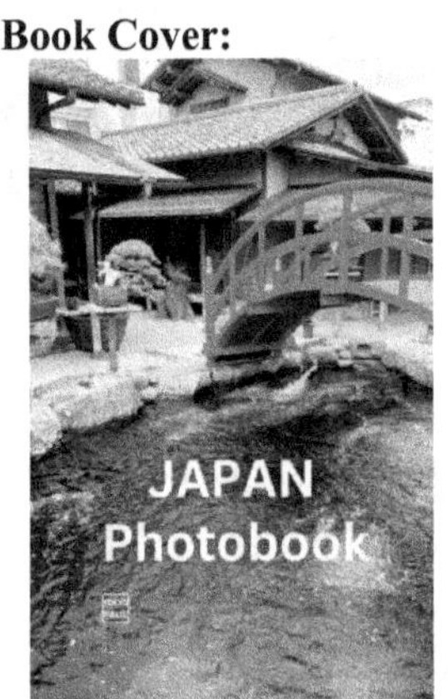


</td></tr>
</table>

# Tokyo Paul's Other Books

**Title:**

Japan Photography Book 2023 Stunning Photos of Japanese Cityscapes, Shrines, Festivals & Nature

**Description:**

Over 75 pages of NEW Stunning Pictures and Photos of Cityscapes, Shrines, Festivals & Nature in this fantastic Japan Photo Book from my YouTube Japan walks. This book is an affordable and cost-effective way to immerse yourself in Japan and see unique sights not seen anywhere else! Experience these breathtaking cities and sights of Japan through amazing photos and be transported to Japan via photos and images in the book; beautiful cityscapes, festival events, and cherry blossoms & illuminations!

**Book Cover:**

# Tokyo Paul's Other Books

| | |
|---|---|
| **Title:**<br>Japan and Its Famous Regional Foods & Things<br><br>**Description:**<br>This comprehensive guidebook explores Japan's rich culture and history through its 47 prefectures. From the bustling streets of Tokyo to the tranquil landscapes of Okinawa, discover each region's unique characteristics and famous attractions. From the historical temples and shrines in Kyoto to the renowned seafood of Hokkaido, this book delves deep into the heart of Japan, detailing the famous regional specialties, delicious local cuisines, and traditional customs of each prefecture. With detailed information, this book is perfect for travelers planning their next trip to Japan and those wanting to deepen their understanding of Japan. | **Book Cover:**<br> |

# Tokyo Paul's Other Books

<table>
<tr><td>

**Title:**

Tokyo Info Guide: Tips & Photos For Traveling in Japan

**Description:**

This book is your best travel companion for discovering Tokyo's lively and diverse cityscape. This thorough guidebook offers in-depth details on the city's history, culture, prominent attractions, helpful advice for navigating the city like a local, and a map of the most popular train line. A valuable tool for first-time tourists, the guidebook also offers essential information on the Japanese language. The Tokyo Guidebook is the ideal travel companion for anyone visiting Tokyo, Japan.

</td><td>

**Book Cover:**

</td></tr>
</table>

# Tokyo Paul's Other Books

**Title:**

Japan Trip Planner (Journal) Kindle Edition

**Description:**

Compact Size: 6 inches by 9 inches

Ample space for writing notes for 10-15 plus trips

Included Sections:

• 100 Must-See Recommendations, 75 Places & 25 Seasonal Events by Popularity

• Budget Log Section

• Checklists: Pre-trip Checklist, Foods Checklist

**Book Cover:**

# About the Author

Tokyo Paul is an Asian American who has lived in Japan for over 7 years. He's lived everywhere, from Osaka to Nagasaki to Toyama to Tokyo in Japan. He enjoys live-streaming videos on YouTube on his channel. He is an avid sushi fan and goes to his favorite sushi restaurant Sushiro every week. He is also on Twitter, Instagram, and Facebook if you wish to follow him for more information about Japan. He has worked as a recruiter in Japan.

Thank you for finishing this book with me. I'm Tokyo Paul. Consider checking me out on YouTube, searching Tokyo Paul to watch my videos about Japan, or any other social media platform such as Facebook, Instagram, and Twitter. Safe journeys, everyone!

The End

www.ingramcontent.com/pod-product-compliance
Lightning Source LLC
Chambersburg PA
CBHW070829250726
48662CB00003B/1142